The Middle

The Middle

Angela Hume

OMNIDAWN PUBLISHING

RICHMOND, CALIFORNIA

2013

Cover art: Nicolas Baier, Pierre de rêve, 2010, ink jet print, 213 x 213 cm.
www.nicolasbaier.com

Cover and interior design by Peter Burghardt

Typefaces: Garamond and ITC Avant Garde Gothic Pro

Offset Printed on
Glatfeler 55# Natures Book Natural (30% PCW) FSC Certified Recycled Paper

Published by Omnidawn Publishing, Richmond, California
www.omnidawn.com   (510) 237-5472   (800) 792-4957
10 9 8 7 6 5 4 3 2 1
ISBN: 978-1-890650-83-4

Thank you to the editors of *Little Red Leaves, Mrs. Maybe,* and *RealPoetik,* in which versions of some of the fragments in this book appear. Sincere thanks to Joseph Lease; to Rusty Morrison, Ken Keegan, and the Omnidawn staff; and to Brenda Hillman for encouragement surrounding this project. Thank you to Evelyn Reilly and Gillian Osborne for offering thoughts on drafts, and to Nathan Brown for suggesting the cover image. Thanks to Nicolas Baier for permission to reproduce "Pierre de rêve."

fragments (one)

all deaths are *violent*

—Tiqqun

—

habitat loss
violet

water   air   ultra
light

radiative
sub-

cut
  aneous

light

we are

forcing
names

...

think   *flesh without*   *figural unity*
(critical body   functions

think   a tumor bu(r)sts
a loose stitch

...

(sub- lethal bio   logical
effects (write

repugnant
that is,

body scuds
across the brown

blown

13

...

a violence   white, a sink of milk
(predicative of

                                              chlorpyrifos
                                              containers for brutal acts

long-term   population-level
impacts

...

end(ocrine
                    disruption

                                                    extractable
wealth

                    (tip
                        the "risk
                    cup"

no starker   health

...

binding   act
    secret   ion

bio
    accumu
lation

(over *virtually all the earth*

(consider the case of maize

...

the canary in the global coal mine

...

the dismantling of a man

better a wounded wilderness than none at all   (we were only ever
                                                                                              none at all

—

including   anxiety
                                   hyper
                         activity:

                                                    (a measure within
          normal range

                         (girl
                                   at
                         risk

artificial
additives

                                                    whose
thought to mimic the effects of   estrogen

          force the dose   (perfect as an egg

...

like: e.g., tossed tissue   try
looking away

try looking away try looking away try looking away try looking away try looking
away try

marked by
stuttering   trembling dizziness nausea intrusion of

nails   a thought

finest pollen   flush   a kind of aka
the season   thisia:

                                        all the windows clapping shut

...

gestational
  BPA
exposure   urine levels   behavioral

       indices
  whose   abstention

whose false
  positive

       (a girl
         gone
       wrong

fragments (two)

in the exercise of violence over life and death more than in any other legal act, law reaffirms itself. But in this very violence something rotten in law is revealed.

—Walter Benjamin

—

private   like a thought
for a wrist   of a thigh

clot   or block

                        crowded out
                        a fist

...

((in the event of an emergency
            there will be

((in the lungs and throat
            dinning

...

first
  demarcate

an aesthetics of
  injury

...

((touch me there
  please

...

first
  ask a name for

this disease

...

the truth that nature
  means in me

...

((grown thick, thick
  with we

no one ever touches us   ...   create no value

—

Blunt
objects   bone   fracture

                    speech centers   leave torn
            human breasts, cleave
                    skulls

(("non-lethal"   rubber wax plastic wood   projectiles

                    loathe the body, own
                        the hema
                        toma

the object's: pain

(all the animals

                    shake
        shake   dialectic of a wound spaced

...

war heaves itself
upon   a wealth of

health

                                        slow sinning, smacks of

(task: locate some evicted
   cut

(inhabit that
   incision

in such a way that can't be used

...

state of pacifi
cation state of

damage state
of destroy all
ex

cess   body
state of little
to no

speech

ill
state

police
state

—

noonish moan, slight
as a relic

(somebody
botched the lawn

want:
immunity

(that is,
ceremony

exception to
exception

(what we want is

...

no
riot, nothing so

holy
(frenzied clutch of

land, a gas
still

born
(coordinated

administered
harm

(cultivate
                                                                  sanctuary

the middle

Now a whole is that which has beginning, middle, and end. A beginning is that which is not itself necessarily after anything else, and which has naturally something else after it; an end is that which is naturally after something itself, either as its necessary or usual consequent, and with nothing else after it; and a middle, that which is by nature after one thing and has also another after it.

—Aristotle

May launches
a rig   drags

wood, shrub

another   purpler
middle term

another clearer
sediment, perigee

moon, over   calm
grown

would you have
wanted your life

to rain   thrash   the drowned
nest

found   man

spruce out back

would you have
taken it   down

snarled in a wire
meant you were twelve

once spirit
was a bone

do you experience

depression   embarrassment   painful

intercourse   hair   a lining

knit of teeth

(spread
  the pack   bring

(water

regret   a dearth
bores   like a drill

only after
a symptom

                                                           makes of
                                                           your body

a middle

or cave   a derelict quiet   the spigot

                    sealed off

casked away   as any oath
a blasphemy

                   profound
                   boredom

on its reel
spinning out

I will (fidelity) but
don't know how to

protect   oneself

                  one body
         means nothing to anything

captive   cry   (ology

                   pressed as
                   middle time:

the temporality
of the middle is

             the temporality of waste

an aesthetics of the middle
dreams in skin   for years

I wasted my body
tight   coil round a hook

without
consequence   the planet

dimming like any
one

encysted, time
spent in such a way

we did not have to   reckon with it

force the middle its

non-ache   ultradian
cycling

                                       most
earthly
condition

for those who
know no earth

in the drift   the middle's
difficulty

                                 wood thrush
point-seven parts   per million

busted birth   nest
                 left

                                     song
                                   gone
neuro
toxins

and so on
through the food chain

rusty blackbird's
forest   litter   second
                               profanation

never a question of
whether   (*also another after*

song   awaiting
                             vocalization

                             awaiting
                           a present

                             a waiting
                       far from whole

1700 miles of   energy security
                                    crosses hundreds of bodies

bit   open fluid pockets
    umen

viscous   omen   (won't flow unless heated
found   diluted

leaking
    crude:

work of the middle   (surfactant

metal hollow (ed-out
foul (ing   air   water   land

                                                                    once

water
f(ol)lowed

when the oil when   the food when
we are well again   will we conceive

a child   crystalline
structures

set to generous   music
                                  (difficult as stopping a

love

from devouring a   sharded
mind

firm   diagnosis

white atmosphere
sick now with snow

                                             awaiting
                                             burial

ask: one in three? one
in five? would you

have done what we did?

when the water
runs out the middle

runs out   until then

iron river   ripped   dark as a
throat

in this summer of   morning

carbon
sink   conifers   combing out the light

road and mill
pulp stink   film

a tongue
scum   somnolent

inside of a house, basically
chlorides, urine   pulse

                          (100000 sq km a day
                              fighting back

ordinary hour
          tracing   now

now   now

goes and
goes

notes

fragments (one)

The epigraph is from the French collective Tiqqun's volume *Introduction to Civil War*.

Some of the language in these fragments is adapted from recent reports on health and environmental research findings, including but not limited to reports published by/at the EPA, Louisiana State University, *Pediatrics*, and www.extinctioncrisis.org.

Page 12: The italicized text is from Adriana Cavarero's book *Horrorism: Naming Contemporary Violence*.

Page 17: Some of the italicized text is from Wallace Stegner's "Wilderness Letter," written to the U.S. Outdoor Recreation Resources Review Commission in 1960.

fragments (two)

The epigraph is from Walter Benjamin's essay "Critique of Violence," which appears in *Reflections*.

Page 27: *the truth that nature / means in me* is from the section of Robert Duncan's *Dante Études* entitled "On Obedience."

The line *no one ever touches us* is from Tiqqun's *Introduction to Civil War*.

Pages 28-32: These fragments were written as response to the October and November 2011 acts of police violence against protestors in Oakland, Berkeley, and Davis, California.

the middle

This series is for J.L.

The epigraph is from Aristotle's *Poetics*.

Some of the language in these fragments is adapted from recent reports on health and environmental findings.

Page 39: It is Hegel who wrote, "the *being of Spirit is a bone*" (see *The Phenomenology of Spirit*).

Page 41: This fragment contains traces of Giorgio Agamben on oath (see his book *The Sacrament of Language*).

Page 45: The lines *would you / have done what we did?* echo Sylvia Plath's "The Hanging Man."

Angela Hume lives in Oakland. She is the author of the chapbook *Second Story of Your Body* (Portable Press at Yo-Yo Labs, 2011). Her poems appear in such journals as *Mrs. Maybe, Little Red Leaves, RealPoetik, eccolinguistics, Zoland Poetry*, and *Spinning Jenny*. A poetics appears in *Evening Will Come*.